HOW&WHY?

ANIMALS GROW NEW PARTS

Elaine Pascoe is the author of more than 20 acclaimed children's books on a wide range of subjects.
Dwight Kuhn's scientific expertise and artful eye work together with the camera to capture the awesome wonder of the natural world.

Please visit our web site at: www.garethstevens.com
For a free color catalog describing Gareth Stevens Publishing's list of high-quality books
and multimedia programs, call 1-800-542-2595 or fax your request to (414) 332-3567.

Library of Congress Cataloging-in-Publication Data

Pascoe, Elaine.
    Animals grow new parts / by Elaine Pascoe; photographs by Dwight Kuhn. — North American ed.
       p. cm. — (How & why: a springboards into science series)
    Includes bibliographical references and index.
    Summary: Explores how and why some animals of the land and sea are able to grow new
body parts.
    ISBN 0-8368-3003-2 (lib. bdg.)
    1. Regeneration (Biology)—Juvenile literature. [1. Regeneration (Biology). 2. Animals.]
I. Kuhn, Dwight, ill. II. Title.
QP90.2.P37   2002
571.8'891—dc21   2001049479

This North American edition first published in 2002 by
Gareth Stevens Publishing
A World Almanac Education Group Company
330 West Olive Street, Suite 100
Milwaukee, WI 53212 USA

First published in the United States in 2000 by Creative Teaching Press, Inc., P.O. Box 2723, Huntington Beach, CA 92647-0723.
Text © 2000 by Elaine Pascoe; photographs © 2000 by Dwight Kuhn. Additional end matter © 2002 by Gareth Stevens, Inc.

Gareth Stevens editor: Mary Dykstra
Gareth Stevens designer: Tammy Gruenewald

Printed in the United States of America

1 2 3 4 5 6 7 8 9 06 05 04 03 02

HOW & WHY?

ANIMALS GROW NEW PARTS

by Elaine Pascoe

photographs by Dwight Kuhn

A SPRINGBOARDS INTO SCIENCE SERIES

Gareth Stevens Publishing

A WORLD ALMANAC EDUCATION GROUP COMPANY

Most starfish are shaped like five-pointed stars, but this starfish looks different. It was attacked by a hungry fish, and three of its arms are gone! Can a starfish survive with only two arms?

Actually, the starfish will not have to live with only two arms. The missing arms will grow back. Before long, the starfish will have all five arms again.

Starfish belong to a small group of animals that have the ability to regenerate. In other words, they can replace lost body parts by growing new ones.

This robin is trying to pull an earthworm out of the ground. The hungry bird gets only part of the worm. Will the worm die?

Maybe not. An earthworm's body has many ringlike segments. The worm needs the first thirty-five segments to live. These segments contain the worm's most important organs. So an earthworm can lose its entire back end. It just grows new segments to replace the ones it lost.

The tiny planarian flatworm is a champion at replacing body parts. If it loses its tail, it grows a new tail. If it loses its head, it grows a new head!

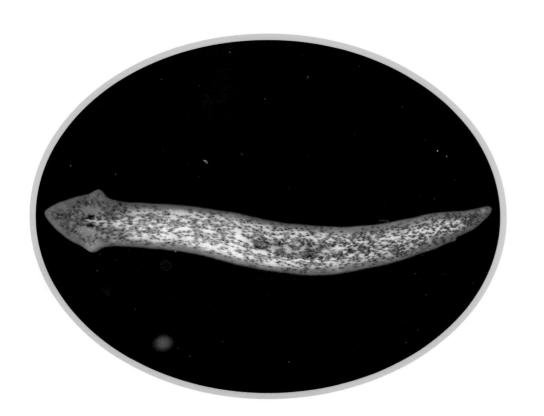

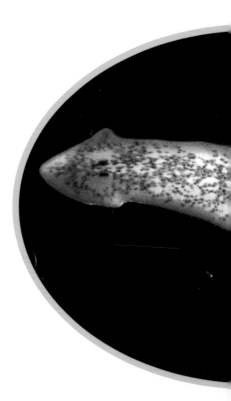

Many animals that grow new parts, such as worms, have simple body structures. But some complex animals can regenerate, too.

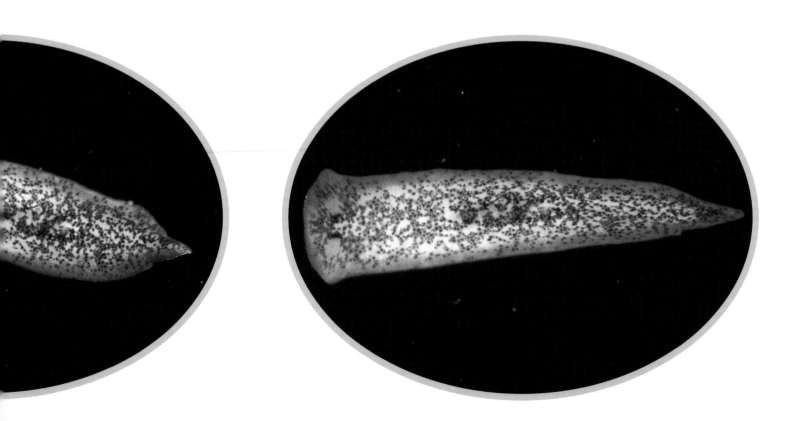

An anole *(uh-**noh**-lee)* lizard is a tasty meal for a bird or some other hungry animal. This lizard, however, can fool its predators with a trick.

When a predator grabs the lizard's tail, the end of the tail breaks off but keeps on wiggling. The wiggling tail fools the predator while the lizard runs away. The lizard soon grows a new tail.

A dragonfly nymph attacks a tadpole and bites its tail. The tadpole struggles to free itself and swims away, leaving its tail behind.

A tadpole's tail grows back quickly. Tadpoles survive many attacks because they are able to lose their tails and grow new ones.

Look carefully at this salamander's leg, just below its feathery gills. Its toes and part of the leg are missing. A fish might have bitten them off — but the salamander escaped.

Before long, the missing leg and toes grow back. The salamander is as good as new!

15

Crayfish and crabs can grow new legs, too. They can also grow new claws. When a crayfish or a crab loses a claw or one of its smaller walking legs, a new part begins to grow immediately.

Regenerating, or growing new parts, is one of the amazing ways crayfish, crabs, and other animals survive.

Can you answer these "HOW & WHY" questions?

1. How can a starfish survive if it loses an arm?

2. Why does an earthworm need the first 35 segments of its body to live?

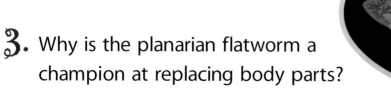

3. Why is the planarian flatworm a champion at replacing body parts?

4. How does an anole lizard fool predators?

5. How does a tadpole survive an attack?

6. How does regeneration help crayfish and crabs?

(See page 20 for answers.)

ANSWERS

1. The starfish grows a new arm through a process called regeneration.

2. An earthworm's most important organs, which are the parts inside that a worm must have to survive, are contained in the first 35 segments of the worm's body.

3. Not only can a planarian flatworm regenerate its tail, but it can also regenerate its head!

4. If a predator grabs an anole lizard's tail, the end of the tail breaks off, and the lizard runs away.

5. When a tadpole is attacked, it can struggle free and swim away, leaving its tail behind.

6. Both crayfish and crabs can survive predators' attacks by growing new legs or claws that are lost during the struggle.

Worm, Sweet, Worm

Earthworms are interesting creatures to watch, but you should keep them only a short time and be very careful not to injure them. To make a temporary worm house, cover the bottom of a large, clear plastic jar with a thick layer of soil. Spray the soil with water, then add a thin layer of sand. Add another thick layer of soil, more sand, and a third layer of soil. Spray each layer of soil and sand with water before adding the next layer. Put a few earthworms into the jar, then add some dead leaves and cover the jar with a cloth. Keep the jar in a dark place. Watch what happens inside your worm house. After a few days, return your wiggly houseguests to the same place you found them.

Be a Cut-Up

Draw a large starfish on a piece of white paper. Draw in some plants, shells, and other scenery, so your picture covers the entire piece of paper. Glue the picture onto some lightweight cardboard. (You could use the front or back of an empty cereal box.) Trim away any cardboard edges, then use a black marker to draw a puzzle pattern onto the picture. Cut apart the puzzle pieces, mix them up, and put the starfish back together.

Crusty Crustaceans

Use books or the Internet to learn all about crabs and crayfish. Make a chart that lists the ways in which they are alike and different. Now add other crustaceans to the chart.

GLOSSARY

attacked: moved toward something or someone in a violent way, trying to cause harm or injury.

champion: someone or something judged to be "the best" in some kind of contest.

claw: the jawlike body part at the end of a crab's or a lobster's front leg, which the animal uses for grasping.

complex: having many parts.

gills: the organs of fish, and most other animals that live in water, which take in oxygen from the water for breathing.

nymph: a young insect that looks almost the same as an adult of its species but has not fully developed into the adult form.

organs: certain parts of an animal's body that have a special use.

planarian flatworm: a small, dark-colored freshwater worm that has a triangular head and a soft, flat body.

predator: an animal that hunts and kills other animals for food.

replace: take the place of someone or something else or put something back in its original place.

segments: the smaller, similar-looking parts that connect to form a larger object.

simple: not having many parts.

struggles: tries very hard.

survive: stay alive.

walking legs: the small legs of a crustacean, such as a crab or a lobster, which the animal uses to move from place to place.

More Books to Read

Crayfish. Early Bird Nature Books (series). Phyllis W. Grimm (Lerner)
It Could Still Be a Worm. Rookie Read-About Science (series). Allan Fowler (Children's Press)
A Salamander's Life. Nature UpClose (series). John Himmelman (Children's Press)
Seashells, Crabs, and Sea Stars. Young Naturalist Field Guides (series).
    Christiane Kump Tibbitts (Gareth Stevens)
Wonderful Worms. Linda Glaser (Millbrook Press)

Videos

GeoKids: Flying, Trying, and Honking Around. (National Geographic)
Tadpoles and Frogs. (National Geographic)
Under the Sea. (Concord Video)

Web Sites

calgarypubliclibrary.com/cya/sra2001/crus.htm
mbgnet.mobot.org/salt/animals/echinod.htm
www.sci.mus.mn.us/sln/tf/w/worms/worms/worms.html

Some web sites stay current longer than others. For additional web sites, use a good search engine to locate the following topics: *anoles, crayfish, earthworms,* and *starfish.*

INDEX